BONUS!

LOOK FOR THE CAMERA in our instructi[...] technique videos made just for you! **www.Leis**[...]

Crochet Refresher

Ease back into crochet with this review of basic techniques (featuring left- and right-handed illustrations) and an exciting collection of designs for baby gifts.

If a new baby is coming into your life, it's only natural to want to make something special for that precious bundle. Now is a great time to get re-acquainted with your long-abandoned crochet skills!

Turn the page for a review of the beginning stitches, with clear illustrations and video links that will help you get back up to speed in no time. The washcloth on page 4 is perfect for practicing these stitches.

Additional stitches and techniques are explained next, so you'll review everything you need to make the fun designs that follow. Parents will appreciate these blankets, baby hat, and mitts, especially if you use easy-care yarn. Just think, your hand-crocheted creations could become tomorrow's heirlooms!

LEISURE ARTS, INC. • Maumelle, Arkansas

Refresher to Beginning Stitches

Here you will find all of the information needed to begin. The washcloth, page 4, is an easy project to make first and practice the beginning stitches.

Remember, you can watch each technique online! www.leisurearts.com/6435

Slip Knot

Pull a length of yarn from the skein and make a circle on top of the yarn that comes from the skein about 6" (15 cm) from the end *(Fig. 1a)*. Slip your hook under the strand in the middle of the circle *(Fig. 1b)*.

Left-handed **Fig. 1a** **Right-handed**

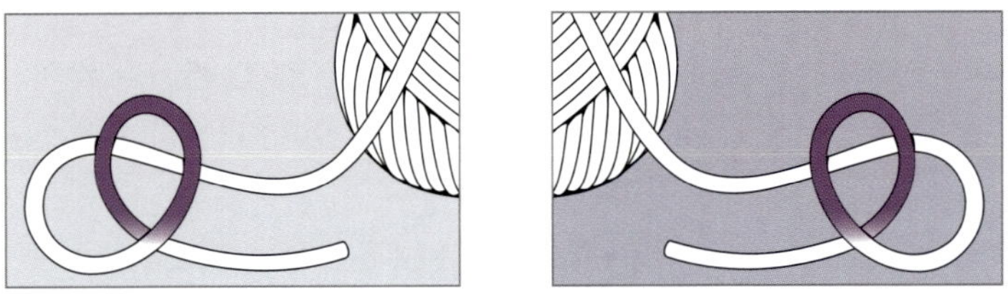

Left-handed **Fig. 1b** **Right-handed**

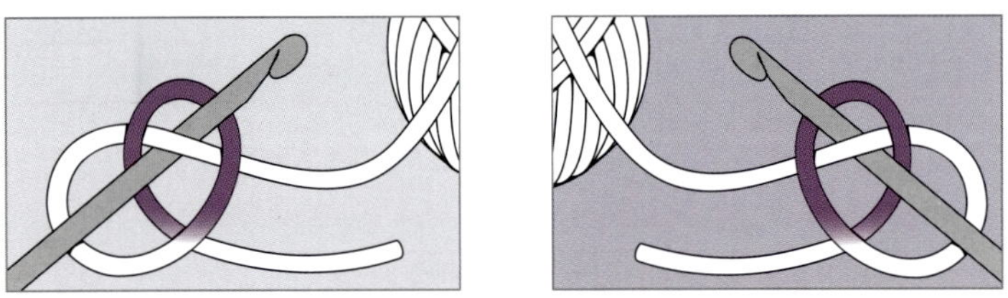

Yarn Over *(abbreviated YO)*

Bring the yarn over the top of the hook from **back** to **front**, catching the yarn with the hook and turning the hook slightly toward you to keep the yarn from slipping off *(Fig. 2)*.

Left-handed **Fig. 2** **Right-handed**

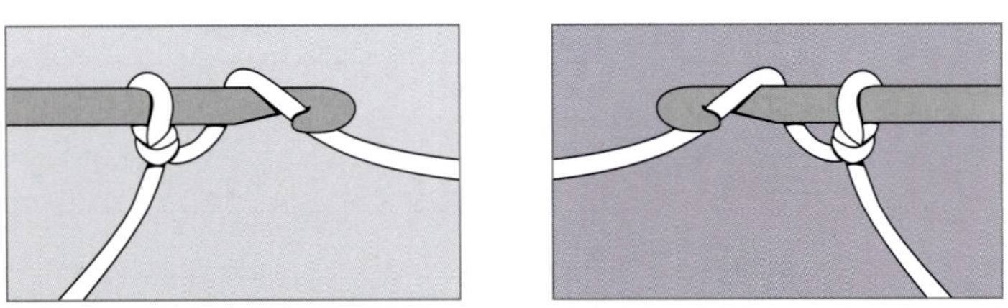

Chain *(abbreviated ch)*

YO and draw the yarn through the loop on the hook *(Figs. 3a & b)*.

Left-handed **Fig. 3a** **Right-handed**

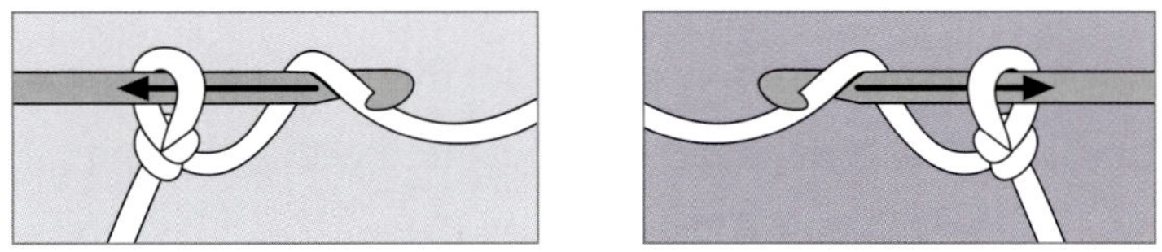

Left-handed **Fig. 3b** **Right-handed**

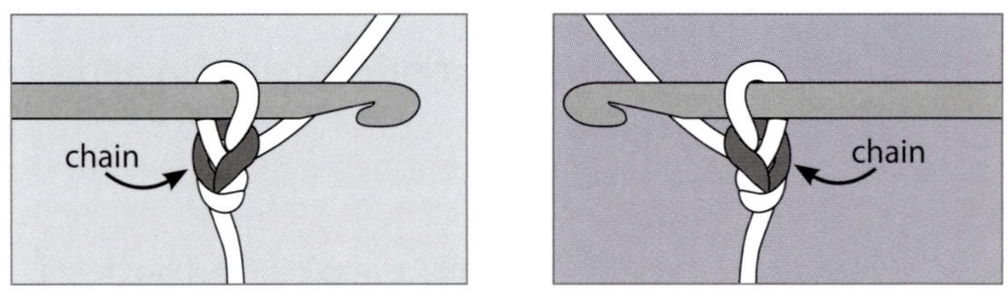

Working in the Chain

Insert hook under the back ridge of each chain *(Fig. 4a)* **or** under the top strand **and** the back ridge *(Fig. 4b)*.

Left-handed **Fig. 4a** **Right-handed**

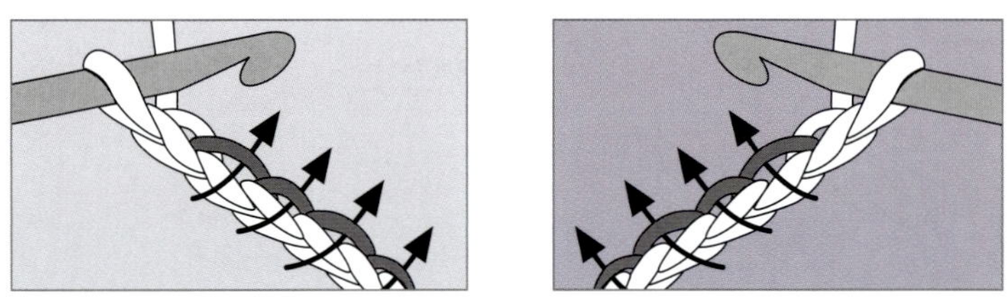

Left-handed **Fig. 4b** **Right-handed**

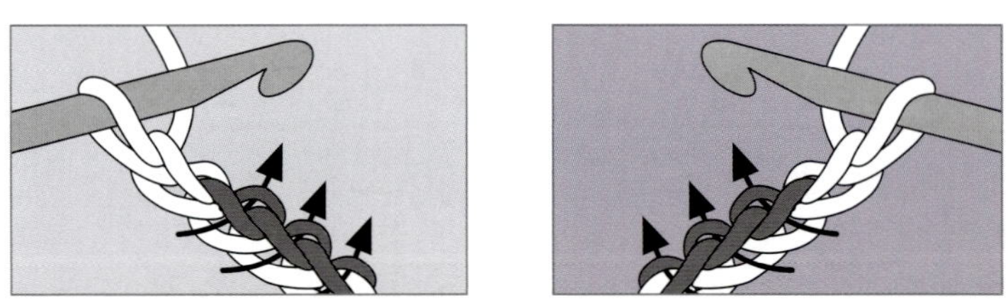

Single Crochet *(abbreviated sc)*

Insert hook in stitch or space indicated, YO and pull up a loop, YO and draw through both loops on hook *(Figs. 5a & b)*.

Left-handed **Fig. 5a** **Right-handed**

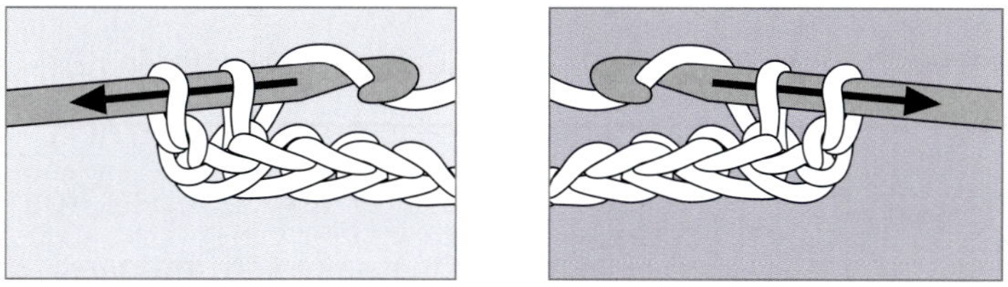

Left-handed **Fig. 5b** **Right-handed**

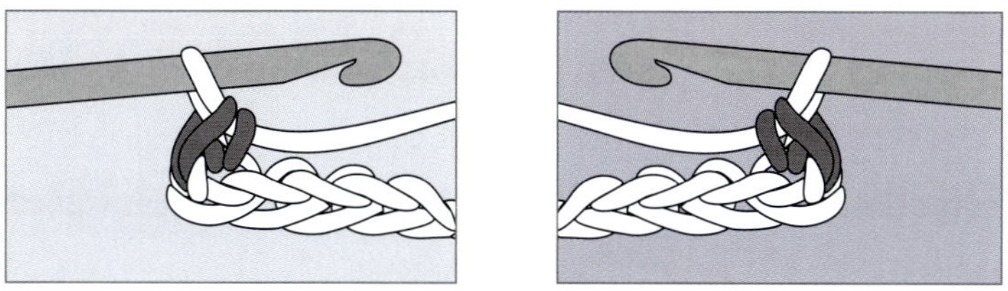

Working in a Stitch

When working in a stitch, insert your hook under **both top loops** of a stitch *(Fig. 6)*, unless otherwise indicated.

Left-handed **Fig. 6** **Right-handed**

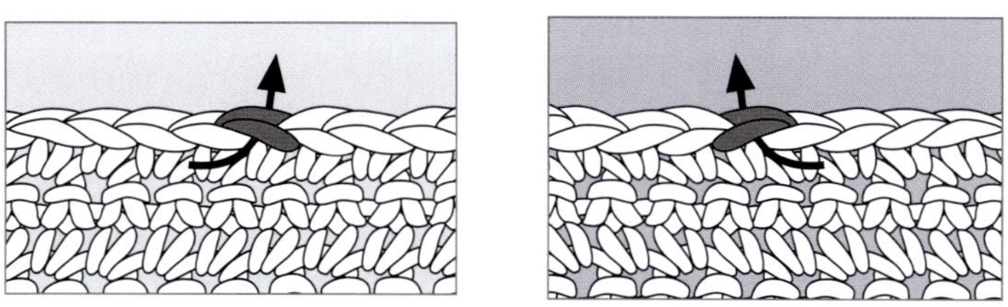

Slip Stitch *(abbreviated slip st)*

Insert hook in stitch indicated, YO and draw through stitch and through loop on hook *(Fig. 7)*.

Left-handed **Fig. 7** **Right-handed**

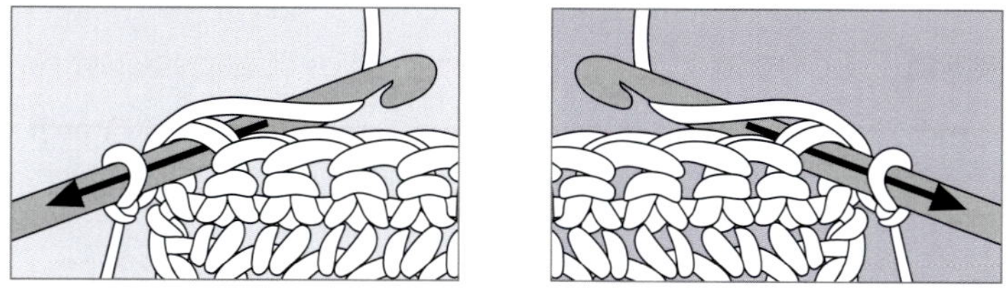

Finish off

Cut yarn leaving an end long enough to weave in. YO and pull yarn completely through loop on hook *(Fig. 8)*; pull the end to tighten the loop.

Left-handed **Fig. 8** **Right-handed**

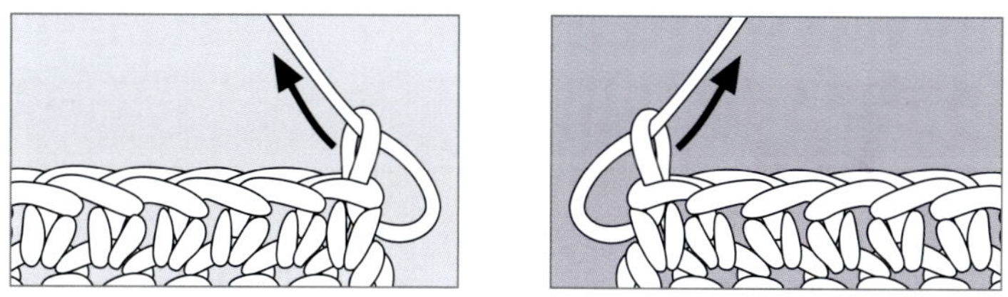

Free Loops

When working an edging, you will be instructed to work in the free loops of the beginning chain. Work in loop indicated by arrow *(Fig. 9)*.

Left-handed **Fig. 9** **Right-handed**

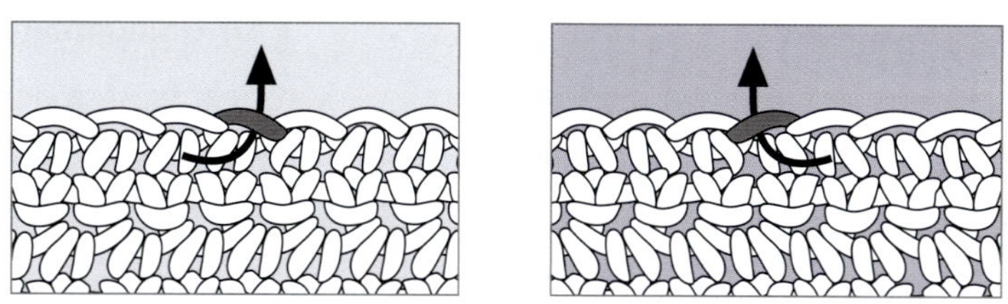

You're on your way to crocheting again! The Refresher to Basic Stitches on page 6 will help you make the remaining projects in this book.

Washcloth

This easy washcloth is an ideal project to make first and ease you into crocheting again. Besides, you can never have too many washcloths with a baby around! Refer to the Refresher to Beginning Stitches on pages 2 and 3.

EASY

Finished Size: Approximately 7" (18 cm) square

SHOPPING LIST

Yarn (Medium Weight Cotton)

[2.5 ounces, 120 yards (71 grams, 109 meters) per skein]:

☐ Solid - 1 skein

[2 ounces, 95 yards (57 grams, 86 meters) per skein]:

☐ Ombre - 1 skein

Yarn Note: Two skeins will make four washcloths: two solid color with an ombre edging and two ombre with a solid edging.

Crochet Hook

☐ Size H (5 mm)

Additional Supplies

☐ Removable markers **or** scrap yarn

☐ Yarn needle

Gauge is not of great importance; your washcloth may be a bit larger or smaller without changing the overall effect.

INSTRUCTIONS

You can make the washcloth with only one color or with two colors, using one of the colors for the Body and the other color for the Edging.

If you need a refresher on abbreviations, symbols, and terms, see page 30.

BODY

Always begin with a slip knot on your hook.

Ch 30; place a marker in first ch from hook to make it easier to find at the end of Row 2.

Row 1: Sc in second ch from hook, ★ ch 1, skip next ch, sc in next ch; repeat from ★ across: 15 sc and 15 chs (counting marked ch).

Row 2: Ch 1, place marker in ch just made, turn; skip first sc, ★ sc in next ch-1 sp, ch 1, skip next sc; repeat from ★ across, sc in marked ch, remove marker: 15 sc and 15 chs.

Continue to place a marker in the turning chain to make it easier to find, until you are comfortable finding the chain without marking it.

Repeat Row 2 for pattern until Body measures approximately 7" (18 cm) from beginning ch.

EDGING

An Edging is worked around the entire piece. You can use the same color as the Body or a contrasting color.

SAME COLOR EDGING

Ch 1, turn; 2 sc in first sc, sc in each ch-1 sp and in each sc across to turning ch, 2 sc in turning ch; sc in end of each row across; working in free loops of beginning ch ***(Fig. 9, page 3)***, 2 sc in first ch, sc in each ch across to corner, 2 sc in corner; sc in end of each row across; join with slip st to first sc, finish off.

CONTRASTING COLOR EDGING

Finish off. Turn work and join Contrasting Color with slip st in first sc; ch 1, 2 sc in same st, sc in each ch-1 sp and in each sc across to turning ch, 2 sc in turning ch; sc in end of each row across; working in free loops of beginning ch *(Fig. 9, page 3)*, 2 sc in first ch, sc in each ch across to corner, 2 sc in corner; sc in end of each row across; join with slip st to first sc, finish off.

Weave in yarn ends with a yarn needle *(Fig. A)*.

Left-handed Fig. A **Right-handed**

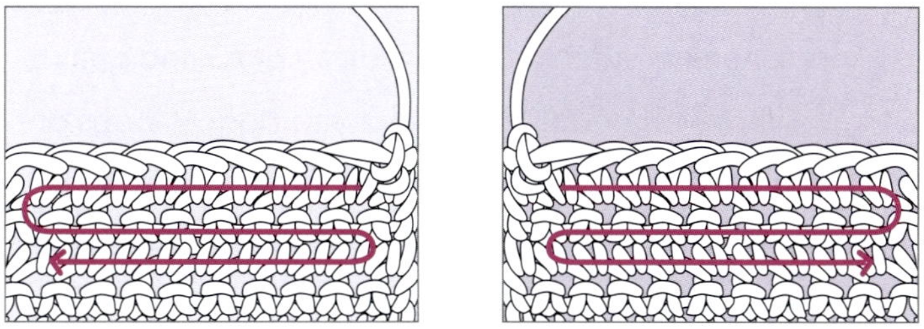

Congratulations! You're crocheting again and you have a washcloth to show for it!

Brush up on more Basic Stitches on pages 6 and 7 so you'll be ready for the remaining projects in this book.

Refresher to Basic Stitches

The following stitches are used in many of the projects in this book. You can refresh your memory by making a practice swatch using all of the basic stitches or wait until you're ready to use them in the project of your choice.

Half Double Crochet *(abbreviated hdc)*

YO, insert hook in stitch indicated, YO and pull up a loop, YO and draw through all 3 loops on hook ***(Figs. 10a & b)***.

Left-handed **Fig. 10a** **Right-handed**

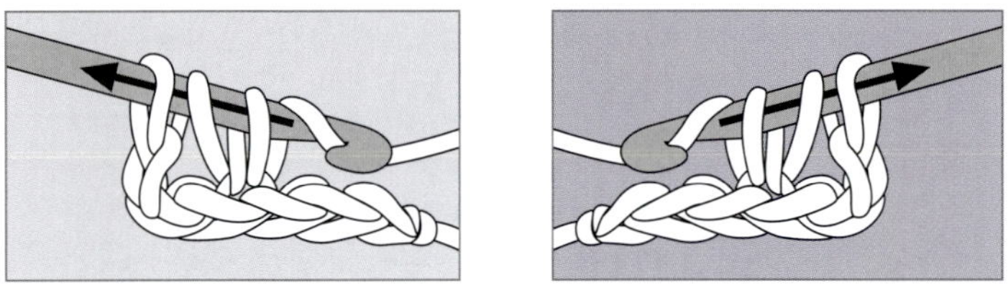

Left-handed **Fig. 10b** **Right-handed**

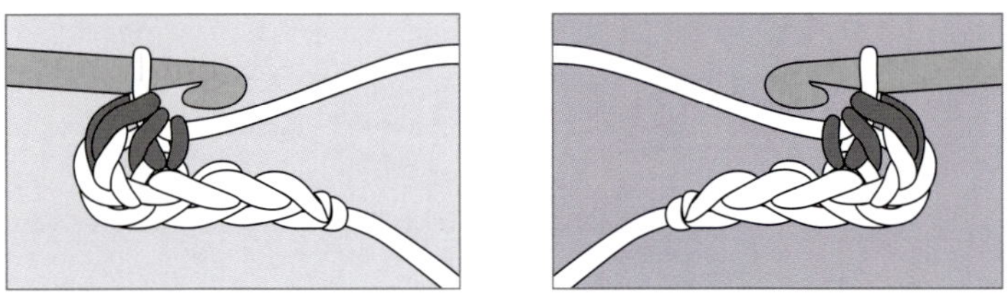

Double Crochet *(abbreviated dc)*

YO, insert hook in stitch or space indicated, YO and pull up a loop (3 loops on hook), YO and draw through 2 loops on hook ***(Fig. 11a)***, YO and draw through remaining 2 loops on hook ***(Fig. 11b)***.

Left-handed **Fig. 11a** **Right-handed**

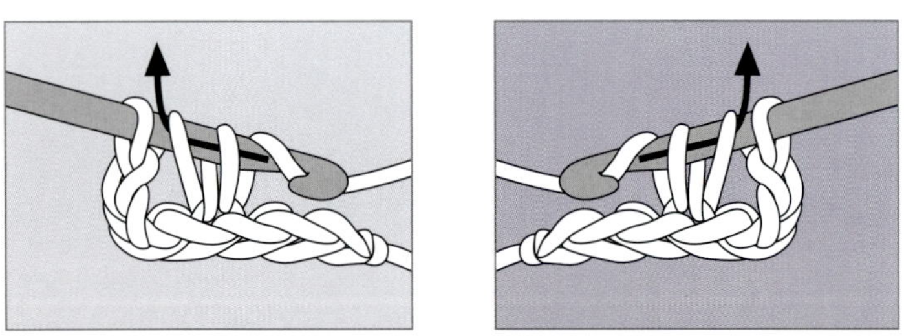

Left-handed **Fig. 11b** **Right-handed**

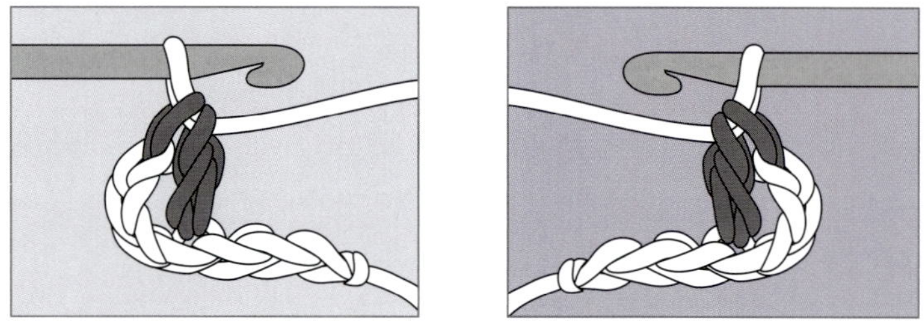

Treble Crochet *(abbreviated tr)*

YO twice, insert hook in stitch or space indicated, YO and pull up a loop (4 loops on hook), (YO and draw through 2 loops on hook) 3 times ***(Figs. 12a & b)***.

Left-handed **Fig. 12a** **Right-handed**

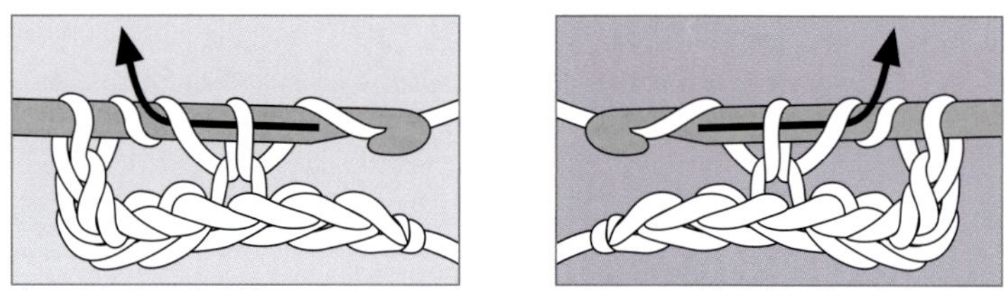

Left-handed **Fig. 12b** **Right-handed**

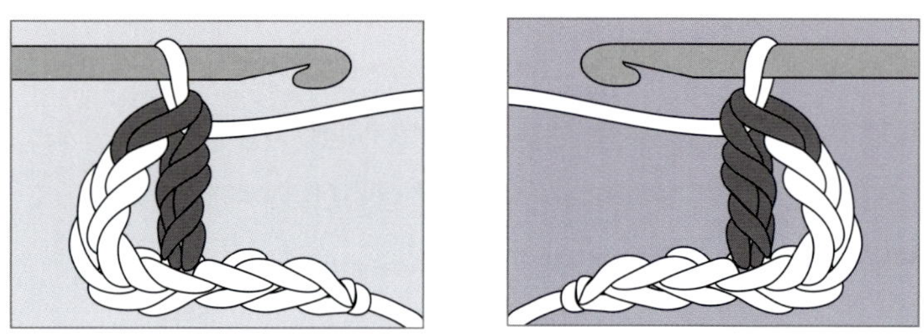

Front Post Double Crochet
(abbreviated FPdc)

YO, insert hook from **front** to **back** around post of stitch indicated ***(Fig. 13a)***, YO and pull up a loop (3 loops on hook), (YO and draw through 2 loops on hook) twice ***(Fig. 13b)***.

Left-handed **Fig. 13a** **Right-handed**

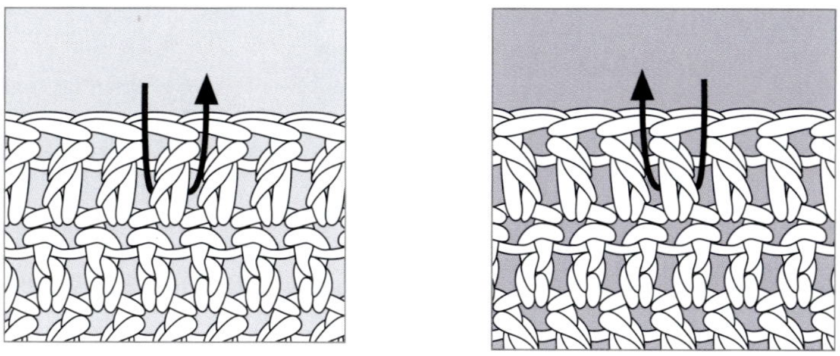

Left-handed **Fig. 13b** **Right-handed**

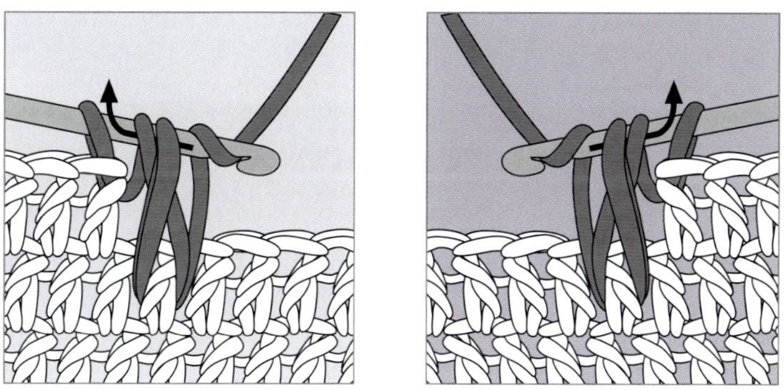

Back Loop

When instructed to work in Back Loop(s) Only, work in loop indicated by arrow ***(Fig. 14)***. The Front Loop left unworked forms a ridge.

Left-handed **Fig. 14** **Right-handed**

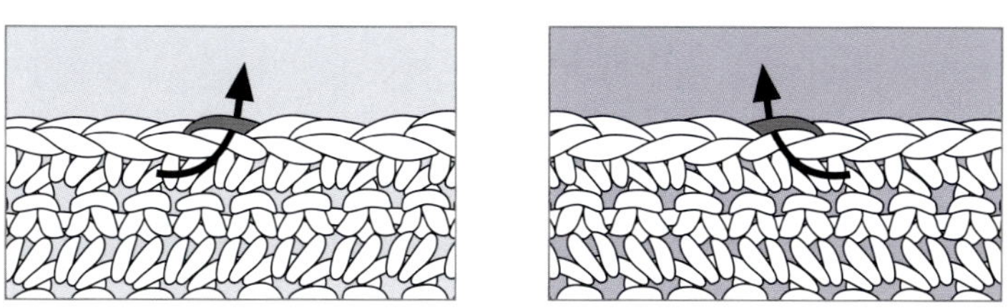

Changing Colors

To change colors while working a sc at the end of a row, insert hook in last sc, YO and pull up a loop, drop yarn; with new color, YO and draw through both loops on hook ***(Fig. 15a)***.

Left-handed **Fig. 15a** **Right-handed**

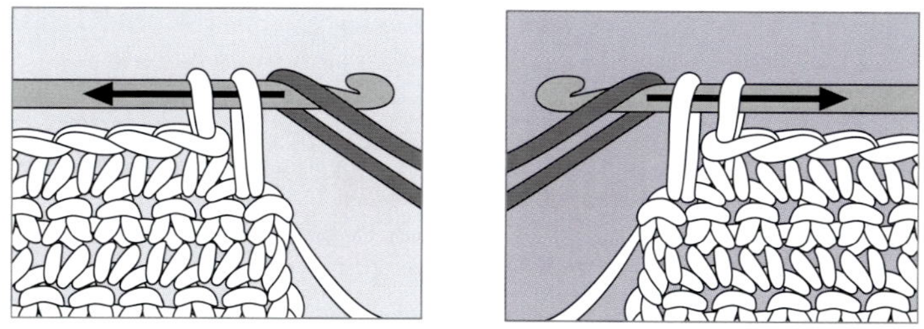

To change colors while working a dc at the end of a row, YO, insert hook in last dc, YO and pull up a loop, YO and draw through 2 loops on hook, drop yarn; with new color, YO and draw through both loops on hook ***(Fig. 15b)***.

Left-handed **Fig. 15b** **Right-handed**

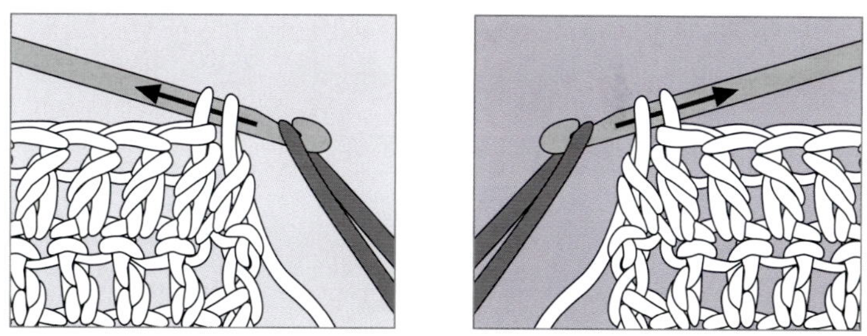

Plaid Blanket

Classic colors are worked in rows of single crochet, then embellished with vertical lines of surface slip stitches to form an overlay chain. It makes a baby blanket that is oh-so-sophisticated.

EASY

Finished Size: 27½" x 30" (70 cm x 76 cm)

SHOPPING LIST

Yarn (Medium Weight) MEDIUM 4
[3.5 ounces, 170 yards (100 grams, 156 meters) per skein]:

- ☐ Tan - 2 skeins
- ☐ Black - 2 skeins
- ☐ White - 1 skein
- ☐ Red - 1 skein

Crochet Hook

- ☐ Size K (6.5 mm) **or** size needed for gauge

Additional Supplies

- ☐ Yarn needle

GAUGE INFORMATION

12 sc and 15 rows = 4" (10 cm)

Gauge Swatch: 4" (10 cm) square

With Tan, ch 13.

Row 1: Sc in second ch from hook and in each ch across: 12 sc.

Rows 2-15: Ch 1, turn; sc in each sc across.

Finish off.

For a refresher on the beginning stitches, see pages 2 and 3.

Technique Used

CHANGING COLORS

To change colors while working a sc at the end of a row, insert hook in last sc, YO and pull up a loop, drop yarn; with new color, YO and draw through both loops on hook *(Fig. 15a, page 7)*.

INSTRUCTIONS

BODY

With Tan, ch 82.

Row 1 (Right side)**:** Sc in second ch from hook and in each ch across: 81 sc.

Note: Loop a short piece of yarn around any stitch to mark Row 1 as **right** side.

Rows 2-9: Ch 1, turn; sc in each sc across.

Row 10: Ch 1, turn; sc in each sc across to last sc, sc in last sc changing to Black; cut Tan.

The rule of thumb is to cut the yarn if it would have to be carried for more than two rows, leaving a long enough yarn end to weave in. Otherwise carry it up the side. The carried strands will be worked over when making the Edging.

It will be easier to work the vertical stripes if you weave in the yarn ends as you go or once you finish the Body.

Repeat Row 2, working in the following color sequence: ★ 2 Rows **each** of Black, (White, Black) twice, 10 rows of Tan; repeat from ★ 4 times **more**.

Finish off.

Instructions continued on page 14.

Stacked Blocks Blanket

Little rectangles make up the building blocks for this neatly geometric blanket, which looks at home in any nursery from classic to contemporary. Chain fringe is integrated into the edging.

EASY

Finished Size: 26½" x 30½" (67.5 cm x 77.5 cm) excluding fringe

SHOPPING LIST

Yarn (Medium Weight) MEDIUM 4
[5 ounces, 256 yards (141 grams, 234 meters) per skein]:
- ☐ 3 skeins

Crochet Hook
- ☐ Size H (5 mm) **or** size needed for gauge

Additional Supplies
- ☐ Yarn needle
- ☐ Removable markers **or** scrap yarn

GAUGE INFORMATION

In pattern,
3 5-dc groups and 8 rows = 3½" (9 cm)

Gauge Swatch: 4¼" wide x 3½" high (10.75 cm x 9 cm)

Ch 19.

Work same as Body Rows 1-8: 3 ch-5 sps.

Finish off.

STITCH GUIDE

For a refresher on the beginning stitches, see pages 2 and 3.

DOUBLE CROCHET ***(abbreviated dc)***

YO, insert hook in st or sp indicated, YO and pull up a loop (3 loops on hook), (YO and draw through 2 loops on hook) twice *(Figs. 11a & b, page 6)*.

INSTRUCTIONS

BODY

Ch 114.

Using a short piece of contrasting color scrap yarn, place a marker in third ch from hook for Edging placement.

Row 1 (Right side)**:** 5 Dc in sixth ch from hook **(5 skipped chs count as first dc plus 2 skipped chs)**, ★ skip next 4 chs, 5 dc in next ch; repeat from ★ across to last 3 chs, skip next 2 chs, dc in last ch: 22 5-dc groups and 2 dc.

Row 2: Ch 1, turn; sc in first dc, ch 5, ★ skip next 5-dc group, sc in sp before next 5-dc group *(Fig. B)*, ch 5; repeat from ★ across to last 5-dc group, skip last 5-dc group, sc in last dc: 22 ch-5 sps.

Fig. B

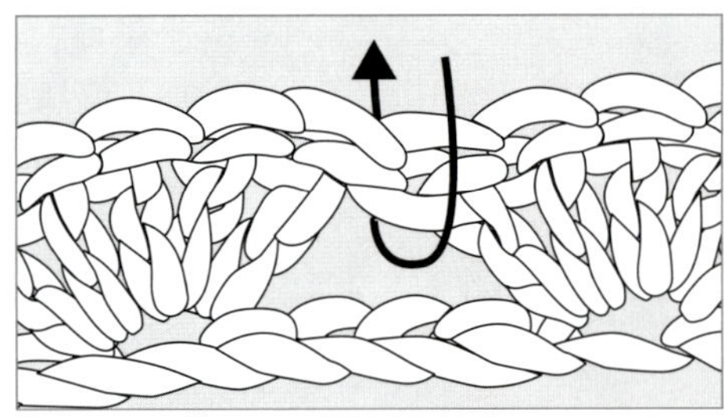

Row 3: Ch 3 **(counts as first dc)**, turn; 5 dc in each ch-5 sp across, dc in last sc: 22 5-dc groups and 2 dc.

Repeat Rows 2 and 3 for pattern until Body measures approximately 30" (76 cm) from beginning ch, ending by working Row 3; do **not** finish off.

Instructions continued on page 15.

Grandma's
baby girl

Circle of Love Blanket

This circular blanket takes on the look of a granny square with a ruffled edge. It's cuddly and comfortable, just like a hug. Use it as a snuggly blanket full size or folded over, or even spread it out as a cozy pallet for baby to rest on.

EASY

Finished Size: 39" (99 cm) diameter

SHOPPING LIST

Yarn (Medium Weight) [MEDIUM 4]

[2.8 ounces, 162 yards (80 grams, 148 meters) per skein**]**:

☐ 6 skeins

Crochet Hook

☐ Size J (6 mm)

or size needed for gauge

Additional Supplies

☐ Yarn needle

GAUGE INFORMATION

In pattern,

(3 dc, ch 1) 3 times and 5 rnds = 3¼" (8.25 cm)

Gauge Swatch: 4" (10 cm) diameter

Work same as blanket through Rnd 3: 12 2-dc groups and 12 ch-1 sps.

If your gauge swatch is the correct size, you can continue working.

STITCH GUIDE

For a refresher on the beginning stitches, see pages 2 and 3.

HALF DOUBLE CROCHET

(abbreviated hdc)

YO, insert hook in tr indicated, YO and pull up a loop, YO and draw through all 3 loops on hook *(Figs. 10a & b, page 6)*.

DOUBLE CROCHET

(abbreviated dc)

YO, insert hook in sp indicated, YO and pull up a loop (3 loops on hook), (YO and draw through 2 loops on hook) twice *(Figs. 11a & b, page 6)*.

TREBLE CROCHET

(abbreviated tr)

YO twice, insert hook in sc indicated, YO and pull up a loop (4 loops on hook), (YO and draw through 2 loops on hook) 3 times *(Figs. 12a & b, page 6)*.

INSTRUCTIONS

Ch 4; join with slip st to form a ring.

Rnd 1: Ch 3 **(counts as first dc, now and throughout)**, dc in ring, ch 1, (2 dc in ring, ch 1) 5 times; join with slip st to first dc: 6 2-dc groups and 6 ch-1 sps.

This blanket is turned at the beginning of each round, making it reversible. Turning puts the hook in a good position to start the next round.

Rnd 2: Turn; slip st in first ch-1 sp, ch 3, dc in same sp, ch 2, (2 dc in next ch-1 sp, ch 2) around; join with slip st to first dc: 6 2-dc groups and 6 ch-2 sps.

Rnd 3: Turn; slip st in first ch-2 sp, ch 3, (dc, ch 1, 2 dc) in same sp, ch 1, (2 dc, ch 1) twice in each ch-2 sp around; join with slip st to first dc: 12 2-dc groups and 12 ch-1 sps.

Circle of Love Blanket

Rnd 4: Turn; slip st in first ch-1 sp, ch 3, 2 dc in same sp, ch 1, (3 dc in next ch-1 sp, ch 1) around; join with slip st to first dc: 12 3-dc groups and 12 ch-1 sps.

Rnd 5: Turn; slip st in first ch-1 sp, ch 3, (dc, ch 1, 2 dc) in same sp, ch 1, (2 dc, ch 1) twice in each ch-1 sp around; join with slip st to first dc: 24 2-dc groups and 24 ch-1 sps.

Rnd 6: Turn; slip st in first ch-1 sp, ch 3, dc in same sp, ch 1, (2 dc in next ch-1 sp, ch 1) around; join with slip st to first dc.

Rnds 7-9: Repeat Rnds 4-6: 48 2-dc groups and 48 ch-1 sps.

Rnds 10-18: Repeat Rnd 4, 9 times: 48 3-dc groups and 48 ch-1 sps.

Rnds 19 and 20: Turn; slip st in first ch-1 sp, ch 3, 3 dc in same sp, ch 1, (4 dc in next ch-1 sp, ch 1) around; join with slip st to first dc: 48 4-dc groups and 48 ch-1 sps.

Rnd 21: Turn; slip st in first ch-1 sp, ch 3, (dc, ch 1, 2 dc) in same sp, ch 1, (2 dc, ch 1) twice in each ch-1 sp around; join with slip st to first dc: 96 2-dc groups and 96 ch-1 sps.

Rnds 22 and 23: Turn; slip st in first ch-1 sp, ch 3, dc in same sp, ch 1, (2 dc in next ch-1 sp, ch 1) around; join with slip st to first dc.

Rnds 24-27: Turn; slip st in first ch-1 sp, ch 3, 2 dc in same sp, ch 1, (3 dc in next ch-1 sp, ch 1) around; join with slip st to first dc: 96 3-dc groups and 96 ch-1 sps.

Rnd 28: Turn; slip st in first ch-1 sp, ch 1, sc in same sp and in each dc and each ch-1 sp around; join with slip st to first sc: 384 sc.

Rnd 29 (Ruffle)**:** Ch 4 (**counts as first tr**), turn; 2 tr in same st as joining, 3 tr in each sc around; join with slip st to first tr.

Rnd 30: Ch 2 (**counts as first hdc**), turn; hdc in next tr and in each tr around; join with slip st to first hdc; finish off.

Weave in yarn ends. Block blanket if desired *(see Blocking, page 31)*.

Plaid Blanket

Continued from page 8.

VERTICAL STRIPES

Vertical stripes are made across the length of the blanket by adding an overlay chain.

To make an overlay chain, hold the specified color on the **wrong** side of the blanket, with **right** side facing, insert hook in sp indicated at bottom of blanket, YO at back of work and draw through blanket ***(Fig. C)***, ★ insert hook in sp on next row, YO at back of work and draw through blanket **and** through loop on hook; repeat from ★ across.

Fig. C

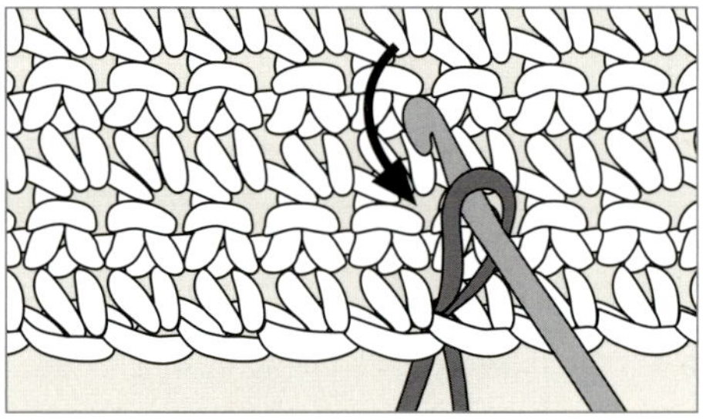

Row 1: With **right** side of blanket facing and using Red, skip first 3 sc on Row 1 of Body and work an overlay chain in next sp (between third and fourth sc) and on each row across length; finish off.

Row 2: Using Black, skip next 4 sc, work an overlay chain in next sp on each row across length; finish off.

Row 3: Using Black, skip next sc, work an overlay chain in next sp on each row across length; finish off.

Row 4: Using Black, skip next 2 sc, work an overlay chain in next sp on each row across length; finish off.

Rows 5-7: Repeat Rows 3 and 4 once, then repeat Row 3 once **more**.

Row 8: Using Red, skip next 4 sc, work an overlay chain in next sp on each row across length; finish off.

Rows 9-36: Repeat Rows 2-8, 4 times.

EDGING

With **right** side facing, join Black with slip st in first sc on last row of Body; ch 1, 3 sc in same st, sc in each sc across to last sc, 3 sc in last sc; sc in end of each row across working around the carried strands (so they do not show); working in free loops of beginning ch *(Fig. 9, page 3)*, 3 sc in first ch, sc in each ch across to last ch, 3 sc in last ch; sc in end of each row across; join with slip st to first sc, finish off.

Weave in yarn ends. Block blanket on **wrong** side if desired *(see Blocking, page 31)*.

Stacked Blocks Blanket

Continued from page 10.

EDGING & CHAIN FRINGE

Chain fringe is made across the top and bottom of the blanket as the Edging is worked.

To make ch fringe, ch 16, slip st in second ch from hook and in each ch across.

Top Edge: Ch 1, turn; sc in first dc, make ch fringe, ★ sc in next 5 dc and in sp **before** next 5-dc group, make ch fringe; repeat from ★ across to last 5-dc group, sc in next 5 dc, make ch fringe, sc in last dc: 23 ch fringes.

First Side Edge: Working around last sc or dc at end of a row, 2 sc around dc on first dc row, ★ sc around next sc, 2 sc around next dc; repeat from ★ across to marker.

Bottom Edge: Sc in marked ch, remove marker, make ch fringe, working in spaces between 5-dc groups and in free loops of chs across bottom edge *(Fig. 9, page 3)*, 5 sc in ch at base of next 5-dc group, ★ sc in next sp, make ch fringe, 5 sc in ch at base of next 5-dc group; repeat from ★ across to last sp, make ch fringe, skip last sp, sc in ch at base of last dc: 23 ch fringes.

Second Side Edge: Working around last sc or dc at end of a row, 2 sc around dc on first dc row, ★ sc around next sc, 2 sc around next dc; repeat from ★ across; join with slip st to first sc, finish off.

Weave in yarn ends. Block blanket if desired *(see Blocking, page 31)*.

Waves Blanket

Gentle waves of color formed by increases and decreases set the stage for a relaxing naptime. Working in the back loops only helps the stripes stand out.

EASY +

Finished Size: 30½" x 36½" (77.5 cm x 92.5 cm)

SHOPPING LIST

Yarn (Medium Weight) 4

[6 ounces, 315 yards (170 grams, 288 meters) per skein]:

- ☐ White - 2 skeins
- ☐ Turquoise - 1 skein

Crochet Hook

- ☐ Size I (5.5 mm) **or** size needed for gauge

Additional Supplies

- ☐ Yarn needle

GAUGE INFORMATION

In pattern,

one repeat (12 sts) = 3¾" (9.5 cm),

6 rows = 4" (10 cm)

Gauge Swatch: 7½" x 4" (19 cm x 10 cm)

With Turquoise, ch 27.

Rows 1 and 2: Work same as Body, page 18: 24 dc.

Rows 3-6: Repeat Row 2, 4 times.

Finish off.

STITCH GUIDE

For a refresher on the beginning stitches, see pages 2 and 3.

DOUBLE CROCHET *(abbreviated dc)*

YO, insert hook in st indicated, YO and pull up a loop (3 loops on hook), (YO and draw through 2 loops on hook) twice *(Figs. 11a & b, page 6)*.

DOUBLE CROCHET 2 TOGETHER *(abbreviated dc2tog)* (uses 2 sts)

★ YO, insert hook in **next** st, YO and pull up a loop, YO and draw through 2 loops on hook; repeat from ★ once **more**, YO and draw through all 3 loops on hook *(Figs. D & E)* **(counts as one dc)**.

Fig. D

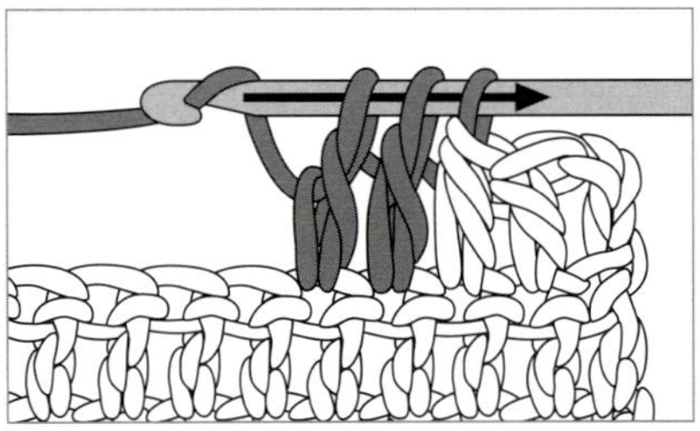

Fig. E

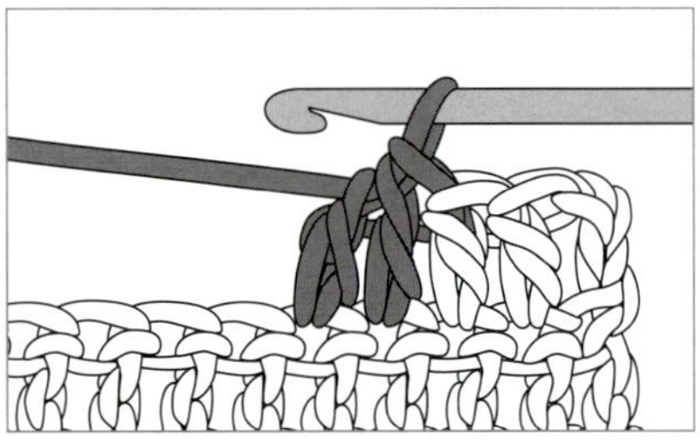

Technique Used

CHANGING COLORS

To change colors while working a dc at the end of a row, YO, insert hook in last dc, YO and pull up a loop (3 loops on hook), YO and draw through 2 loops on hook, drop yarn; with new color, YO and draw through both loops on hook *(Fig. 15b, page 7)*.

INSTRUCTIONS

BODY

Ch 99.

Row 1 (Right side)**:** Dc in fourth ch from hook (**3 skipped chs count as first dc**) and in next 3 chs, dc2tog twice, dc in next 3 chs, ★ 2 dc in each of next 2 chs, dc in next 3 chs, dc2tog twice, dc in next 3 chs; repeat from ★ across to last ch, 2 dc in last ch: 96 dc.

Note: Loop a short piece of yarn around any stitch to mark Row 1 as **right** side.

Row 2: Ch 3 (**counts as first dc, now and throughout**), turn; working in Back Loops Only *(Fig. 14, page 7)*, dc in first 4 dc, dc2tog twice, dc in next 3 dc, ★ 2 dc in each of next 2 dc, dc in next 3 dc, dc2tog twice, dc in next 3 dc; repeat from ★ across to last dc, 2 dc in last dc.

Rows 3-5: Repeat Row 2, 3 times.

Row 6: Ch 3, turn; working in Back Loops Only, dc in first 4 dc, dc2tog twice, dc in next 3 dc, ★ 2 dc in each of next 2 dc, dc in next 3 dc, dc2tog twice, dc in next 3 dc; repeat from ★ across to last dc, dc in last dc, dc in same dc changing to Turquoise; cut White.

The rule of thumb is to cut the yarn if it would have to be carried for more than two rows, leaving a long enough yarn end to weave in. Otherwise carry it up the side. The carried strands will be worked over when making the Edging.

Changing colors in same manner, repeat Row 2 for pattern working in the following color sequence: ★ 6 Rows Turquoise, 6 rows White, 2 rows Turquoise, 2 rows White, 2 rows Turquoise, 6 rows White; repeat from ★ once **more**. Do **not** change colors at end of last row; finish off.

EDGING

With **right** side facing, join Turquoise with slip st in first dc on last row; ch 1, 3 sc in same st, sc in each dc across to last dc, 3 sc in last dc; sc evenly across end of rows; working in free loops of beginning ch *(Fig. 9, page 3)*, 3 sc in first ch, sc in each ch across to ch at base of last dc, sc in next ch, 3 sc in next ch; sc evenly across end of rows working around carried strands; join with slip st to first sc, finish off.

Weave in yarn ends. Block blanket if desired *(see Blocking, page 31)*.

Flowers & Stars Blanket

The colorful flower motifs in this cheerful blanket are joined as you make them, with chain stitch stars added at the end to fill in between the motifs.

Shown on page 21.

INTERMEDIATE

Finished Size: 30" x 36" (76 cm x 91.5 cm)

SHOPPING LIST

Yarn (Medium Weight) MEDIUM 4

[5 ounces, 256 yards (141 grams, 234 meters) per skein]:

- ☐ White - 2 skeins

[4 ounces, 204 yards (113 grams, 187 meters) per skein]:

- ☐ Blue Ombre - 1 skein
- ☐ Pink Ombre - 1 skein
- ☐ Green Ombre - 1 skein

Crochet Hook

- ☐ Size I (5.5 mm) **or** size needed for gauge

Additional Supplies

- ☐ Yarn needle

GAUGE INFORMATION

Flower Motif = 6" (15.25 cm) diameter
Gauge Swatch: 4" (10 cm) diameter
Work same as Motif through Rnd 3: 32 dc, 8 FPdc, and 8 ch-3 sps.
If your gauge swatch is the correct size, you can continue working the Motif.

STITCH GUIDE

For a refresher on the beginning stitches, see pages 2 and 3.

DOUBLE CROCHET *(abbreviated dc)*
YO, insert hook in sp indicated, YO and pull up a loop (3 loops on hook), (YO and draw through 2 loops on hook) twice *(Figs. 11a & b, page 6)*.

TREBLE CROCHET *(abbreviated tr)*
YO twice, insert hook in sc indicated, YO and pull up a loop (4 loops on hook), (YO and draw through 2 loops on hook) 3 times *(Figs. 12a & b, page 6)*.

FRONT POST DOUBLE CROCHET *(abbreviated FPdc)*
YO, insert hook from **front** to **back** around post of tr indicated, YO and pull up a loop (3 loops on hook), (YO and draw through 2 loops on hook) twice *(Figs. 13a & b, page 7)*. Skip tr behind FPdc.

INSTRUCTIONS

FIRST MOTIF

With Blue Ombre, ch 4; join with slip st to form a ring.

Rnd 1 (Right side)**:** Ch 1, 8 sc in ring; join with slip st to first sc.

Note: Loop a short piece of yarn around any stitch to mark Rnd 1 as **right** side.

Rnd 2: Ch 7 **(counts as first tr plus ch 3)**, (tr in next sc, ch 3) around; join with slip st to first tr (fourth ch of turning ch-7): 8 tr and 8 ch-3 sps.

Rnd 3: Slip st in first ch-3 sp, ch 3 **(counts as first dc, now and throughout)**, (dc, ch 3, 2 dc) in same sp, work FPdc around next tr, ★ (2 dc, ch 3, 2 dc) in next ch-3 sp, work FPdc around next tr; repeat from ★ around; join with slip st to first dc, finish off: 32 dc, 8 FPdc, and 8 ch-3 sps.

Rnd 4: With **right** side facing, join White with slip st in any ch-3 sp; ch 3, 8 dc in same sp, skip next 2 dc, sc in next FPdc, skip next 2 dc, ★ 9 dc in next ch-3 sp, skip next 2 dc, sc in next FPdc, skip next 2 dc; repeat from ★ around; join with slip st to first dc, finish off: 8 9-dc groups and 8 sc.

Weave in yarn ends after each Motif is made to keep your project neat and prevent it from being a big task at the end of your project.

NO-SEW JOINING

The method used to connect the Motifs is a no-sew joining also known as "join-as-you-go." After the First Motif is made, each remaining Motif is worked through Rnd 3, then crocheted together as Rnd 4 is worked. Holding Motifs with **wrong** sides together, work slip st into stitch as indicated *(Fig. F)*.

Fig. F

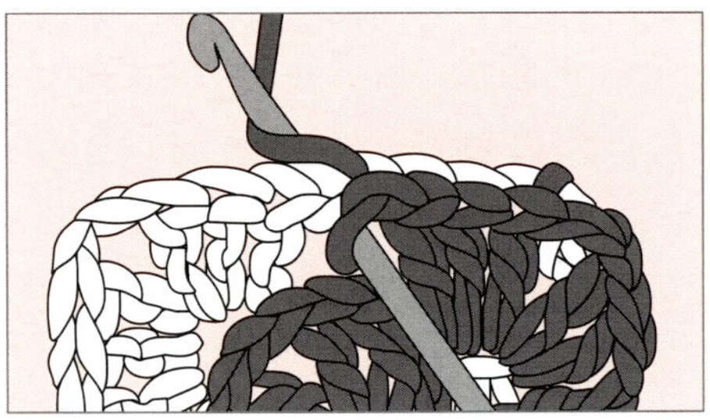

REMAINING MOTIFS

Follow Placement Chart for next color to use.

ONE SIDE JOINING

Work same as First Motif through Rnd 3: 32 dc, 8 FPdc, and 8 ch-3 sps.

Rnd 4: With **right** side facing, join White with slip st in any ch-3 sp; ch 3, 8 dc in same sp, skip next 2 dc, sc in next FPdc, ★ skip next 2 dc, 9 dc in next ch-3 sp, skip next 2 dc, sc in next FPdc; repeat from ★ 4 times **more**, † skip next 2 dc, 4 dc in next ch-3 sp, slip st in fifth dc of 9-dc group on **corresponding Motif**, 5 dc in same sp on **new Motif**, skip next 2 dc, sc in next FPdc †, repeat from † to † once, skip last 2 dc; join with slip st to first dc, finish off: 8 9-dc groups and 8 sc.

TWO SIDE JOINING

Work same as First Motif through Rnd 3: 32 dc, 8 FPdc, and 8 ch-3 sps.

Rnd 4: With **right** side facing, join White with slip st in any ch-3 sp; ch 3, 8 dc in same sp, skip next 2 dc, sc in next FPdc, ★ skip next 2 dc, 9 dc in next ch-3 sp, skip next 2 dc, sc in next FPdc; repeat from ★ 2 times **more**, † skip next 2 dc, 4 dc in next ch-3 sp, slip st in fifth dc of 9 dc group on **corresponding Motif**, 5 dc in same sp on **new Motif**, skip next 2 dc, sc in next FPdc †, repeat from † to † 3 times **more**, skip last 2 dc; join with slip st to first dc, finish off: 8 9-dc groups and 8 sc.

PLACEMENT CHART

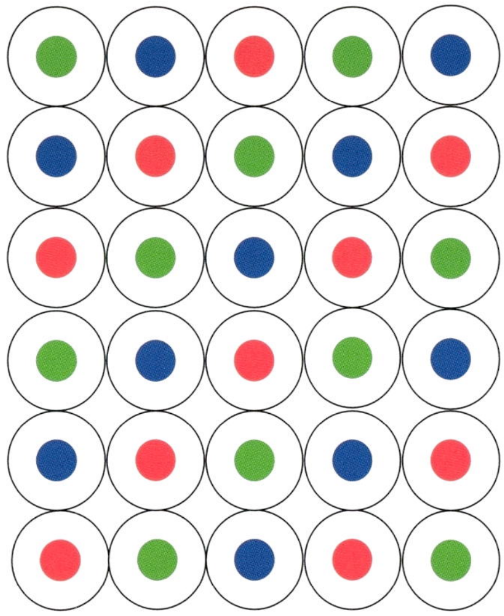

STAR

With White, ch 4; join with slip st to form a ring.

Rnd 1: Ch 1, 8 sc in ring; join with slip st to first sc.

The next round joins the Star to the space between four Motifs.

Rnd 2: ★ Ch 4, with **right** side facing, slip st in sc between 2 9-dc groups on **corresponding Motif**, ch 4, slip st in next sc on **Star**, ch 4, slip st in joined point between 2 **Motifs**, ch 4, slip st in next sc on **Star**; repeat from ★ around working last slip st in same sc at base of first ch-4; finish off.

Make a Star in each space between Motifs.

Weave in yarn ends. Block blanket if desired *(see Blocking, page 31)*.

Baby Hat

The brim of this sweet little hat is worked sideways to create ribbing. Post stitches on the body create the illusion that there are two colors used on each row, when it's actually just one color. Pom-poms finish the hat with a flourish.

Infant size shown on page 27.

INTERMEDIATE

SHOPPING LIST

Yarn (Medium Weight) MEDIUM 4

[6 ounces, 315 yards (170 grams, 288 meters) per skein]:

- ☐ Cream - 1 skein
- ☐ Black - 1 skein

Crochet Hooks

- ☐ Size G (4 mm) **and**
- ☐ Size I (5.5 mm)

or sizes needed for gauge

Additional Supplies

- ☐ Yarn needle
- ☐ Removable markers or scrap yarn
- ☐ Cardboard - 4" x 7" (10 cm x 18 cm)

SIZE INFORMATION

Finished Sizes:

Infant: 14¼" (36 cm) circumference

Toddler: 16½" (42 cm) circumference

Size Note: We have printed the instructions for the sizes in different colors to make it easier for you to find:

- Infant in Blue
- Child in Pink

Instructions in Black apply to both sizes.

GAUGE INFORMATION

In Ribbing, with larger size hook,
12 sts = 3¼" (8.25 cm),
8 rows = 3" (7.5 cm)

Note: Row gauge for the Ribbing is very important since it determines the finished circumference.

In Body pattern, with smaller size hook, 9 sts = 2½" (6.25 cm)

Gauge Swatch: 3¼" wide x 3" high (8.25 cm x 7.5 cm)

With Cream, ch 13.

Work same as Ribbing Rows 1-8, page 24: 12 sts.

For Infant Size, if your gauge is the correct size, you can continue to work Ribbing; for Toddler Size, finish off.

STITCH GUIDE

For a refresher on the beginning stitches, see pages 2 and 3.

HALF DOUBLE CROCHET

(abbreviated hdc)

YO, insert hook in st indicated, YO and pull up a loop, YO and draw through all 3 loops on hook *(Figs. 10a & b, page 6)*.

DOUBLE CROCHET

(abbreviated dc)

YO, insert hook in st indicated, YO and pull up a loop (3 loops on hook), (YO and draw through 2 loops on hook) twice *(Figs. 11a & b, page 6)*.

FRONT POST DOUBLE CROCHET

(abbreviated FPdc)

YO, insert hook from **front** to **back** around post of dc indicated, YO and pull up a loop (3 loops on hook), (YO and draw through 2 loops on hook) twice *(Figs. 13a & b, page 7)*.

Technique Used

CHANGING COLORS

To change colors while working a dc at the end of a row, YO, insert hook in last sc, YO and pull up a loop (3 loops on hook), YO and draw through 2 loops on hook, drop yarn; with new color, YO and draw through both loops on hook *(Fig. 15b, page 7)*. Do **not** cut yarn.

INSTRUCTIONS

RIBBING

The Ribbing is worked to the circumference of the hat and will be folded in half lengthwise to form a brim.

Using larger size hook and Cream, ch 13{17}; place a marker in first ch from hook to make it easier to find at the end of Row 2.

Row 1: Hdc in third ch from hook **(2 skipped chs count as first hdc)** and in each ch across: 12{16} hdc.

Row 2: Ch 1, turn; sc in Back Loop Only of each hdc across *(Fig. 14, page 7)* including marked st; remove marker.

Row 3: Ch 2 **(counts as first hdc)**, place marker in last ch made, turn; hdc in Back Loop Only of next sc and each sc across.

Continue to place a marker in the turning chain-2 to make it easier to find, until you are comfortable finding the chain without marking it.

Rows 4 thru 38{44}: Repeat Rows 2 and 3, 17{20} times; then repeat Row 2 once **more**.

BODY

Change to smaller size hook.

Beginning by working across length of Ribbing, the hat is worked flat and seamed up the back.

Row 1: Ch 1, working across end of rows, sc in first sc row, 2 sc in next hdc row, (sc in next sc row, 2 sc in next hdc row) across: 57{66} sc.

Row 2: Ch 3 **(counts as first dc)**, turn; dc in next sc and in each sc across to last sc, dc in last sc changing to Black.

Carry the unused yarn up the side. The carried strands will be hidden when sewing the seam.

Row 3 (Right side)**:** Ch 1, turn; sc in first dc, work FPdc around next dc, ★ sc in next 2 dc, work FPdc around next dc; repeat from ★ across to last dc, sc in last dc: 19{22} FPdc and 38{44} sc.

Row 4: Ch 3, turn; dc in next st and in each st across to last sc, dc in last sc changing to Cream: 57{66} dc.

When working a FPdc on the following rows, pull up a loop even with the loop on the hook, making the FPdc the same height as the sc.

Row 5: Ch 1, turn; sc in first dc, work FPdc around FPdc in row **below** next dc, skip dc **behind** FPdc just made, ★ sc in next 2 dc, work FPdc around FPdc in row **below** next dc, skip dc **behind** FPdc just made; repeat from ★ across to last dc, sc in last dc: 19{22} FPdc and 38{44} sc.

Row 6: Ch 3, turn; dc in next st and in each st across to last sc, dc in last sc changing to next color: 57{66} dc.

Rows 7 thru 16{20}: Repeat Rows 5 and 6, 5{7} times.

Cut Cream leaving a long end for sewing. Finish off Black.

Fold the Body in half with **right** side together, matching end of rows. Using Cream, whipstitch *(Figs. G & H, page 25)* across Body making sure that the carried strands don't show on the right side, then whipstitch across Ribbing. Fold the Ribbing in half to the **wrong** side matching the bottom edge to Row 1 of the Body; sew in place.

Flatten the Hat with **wrong** side together and the seam centered at the back. Using Cream, whipstitch top seam allowing the stitching to show.

Technique Used

WHIPSTITCH

With **right** sides together, sew through both pieces once to secure the beginning of the seam. Insert the needle from **back** to **front** through **both** loops of each stitch on **both** pieces *(Fig. G)*, **or** in end of rows *(Fig. H)*. Bring the needle around and insert it from **back** to **front** through the next strands on both pieces. Continue in same manner, keeping the sewing yarn fairly loose.

Fig. G

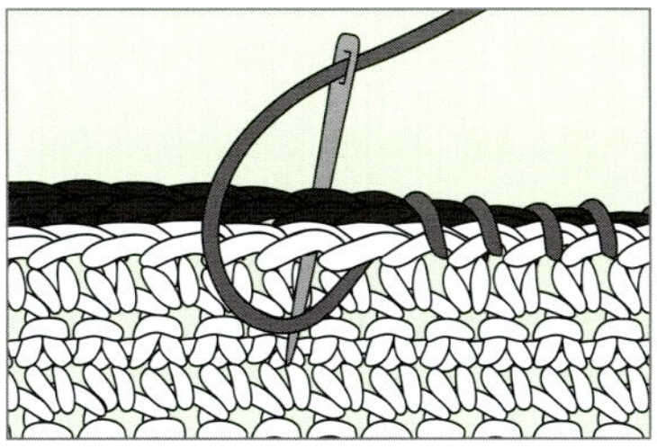

Fig. H

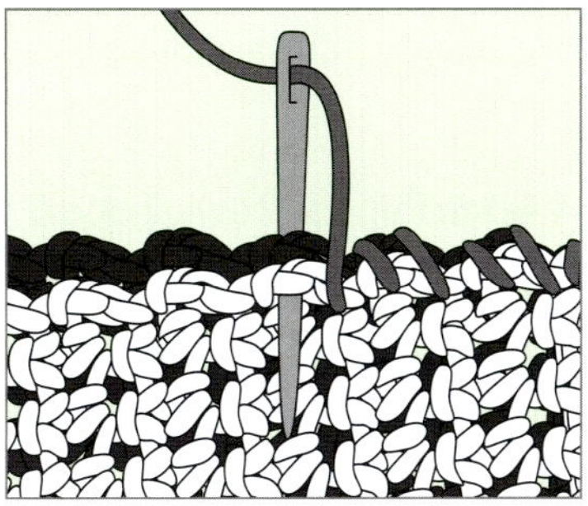

POM-POM (Make 2)

Cut 2 cardboard circles using pom-pom pattern.

Cut a 36" (91.5 cm) length of Black. Fold the strand in half and place it between the two cardboard circles.

Holding one strand of each color together, wind the yarn around the cardboard circle at least 30 times *(Fig. I)*.

Fig. I

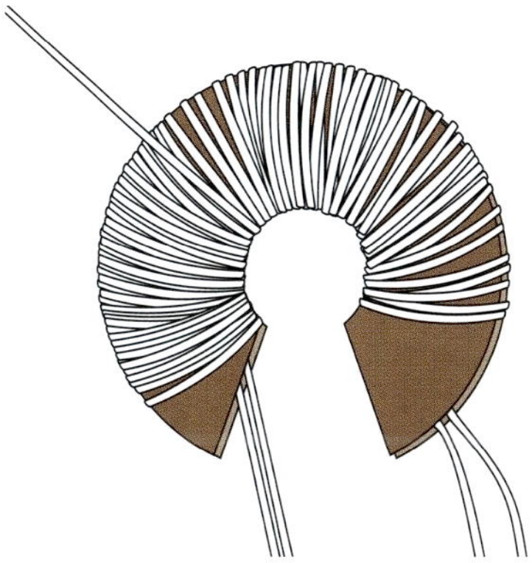

Insert sharp scissors between the cardboard circles and cut the yarn along the outer edge *(Fig. J)*, being careful to keep the pieces of yarn from falling off the cardboard.

Fig. J

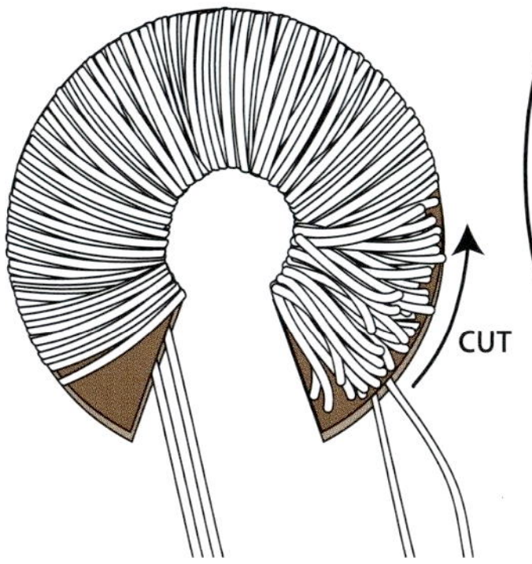

Tie a double knot with the 36" (91.5 cm) strand *(Fig. K)*, making sure it's very tight. Move the strands around to the opposite side of the first knot and tie another double knot.

Gently remove the cardboard circles. Fluff the pom-pom into a ball and trim the ends.

Fig. K

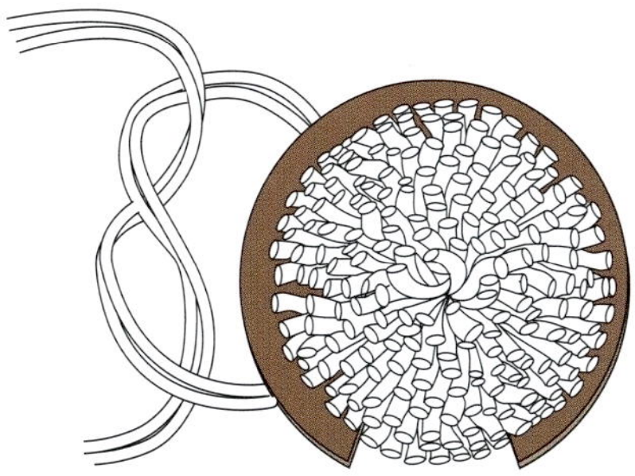

Placing each pom-pom on a corner of the hat, pull the ends to the wrong side a few stitches apart and tie the ends together; secure in place.

Weave in yarn ends.

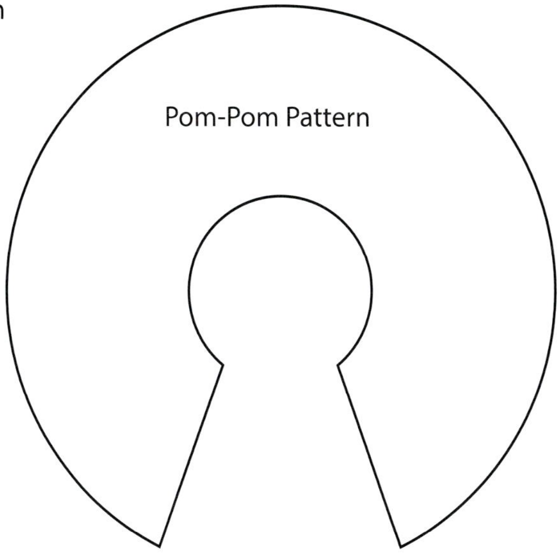

Baby Mitts

Keep teeny fingers warm with these toasty mittens. Ribbed cuffs have plenty of length to help keep them on baby's hands. Pair these with the Hat on page 22 for a perfect winter set.

INTERMEDIATE

Finished Size: 4¾" long x 5½" circumference (12 cm x 14 cm)

SHOPPING LIST

Yarn (Medium Weight) 4

[6 ounces, 315 yards (170 grams, 288 meters) per skein]:

- ☐ Cream - 1 skein
- ☐ Black - small amount

Crochet Hook

- ☐ Size G (4 mm) **or** size needed for gauge

Additional Supplies

- ☐ Yarn needle
- ☐ Removable markers **or** scrap yarn

GAUGE INFORMATION

In Ribbing,

9 sts and 6 rows = 2" (5 cm)

Gauge Swatch: 2" (5 cm) square

Work same as Ribbing through Row 6.

STITCH GUIDE

For a refresher on the beginning stitches, see pages 2 and 3.

HALF DOUBLE CROCHET ***(abbreviated hdc)***

YO, insert hook in st indicated, YO and pull up a loop, YO and draw through all 3 loops on hook *(Figs. 10a & b, page 6)*.

SINGLE CROCHET 2 TOGETHER ***(abbreviated sc2tog)*** (uses 2 sc)

Pull up a loop in each of next 2 sc, YO and draw through all 3 loops on hook *(Figs. L & M)* **(counts as one sc)**.

Fig. L

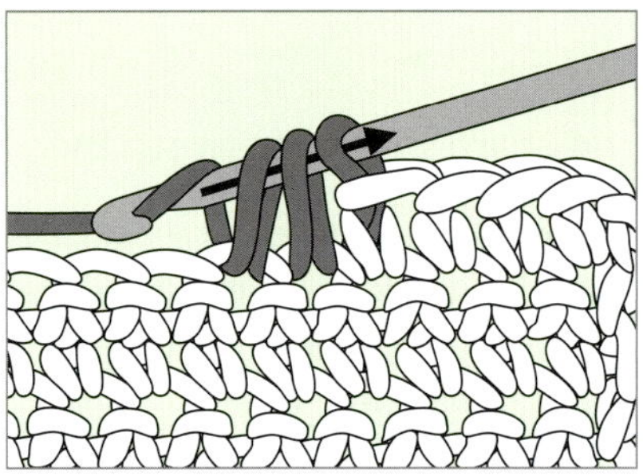

Fig. M

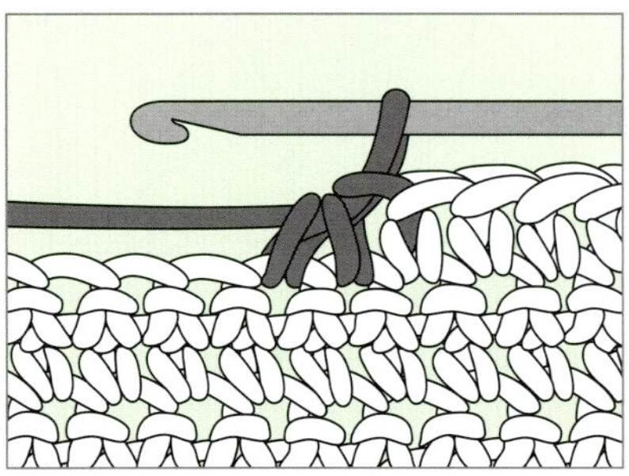

INSTRUCTIONS

RIBBING

With Cream, ch 10; place a marker in first ch from hook to make it easier to find at the end of Row 2.

Row 1 (Right side)**:** Hdc in third ch from hook **(2 skipped chs count as first hdc)** and in each ch across: 9 hdc.

Note: Loop a short piece of yarn around any stitch to mark Row 1 as **right** side.

Row 2: Ch 1, turn; sc in Back Loop Only of each hdc across *(Fig. 14, page 7)* including marked st; remove marker.

Row 3: Ch 2 **(counts as first hdc)**, place marker in last ch made, turn; hdc in Back Loop Only of next sc and each sc across.

Continue to place a marker in the turning chain-2 to make it easier to find, until you are comfortable finding the chain without marking it.

Rows 4-16: Repeat Rows 2 and 3, 6 times; then repeat Row 2 once **more**.

Joining Row: Turn; fold Ribbing in half with **right** side together and matching sts on last row to beginning ch; working through **both** layers, slip st in both loops of each st across; do **not** finish off.

Turn Ribbing right side out.

BODY

Begin working in rounds.

Rnd 1 (Right side)**:** Ch 1, working across end of rows, 2 sc in first sc row, sc in next hdc row, (2 sc in next sc row, sc in next hdc row) around; do **not** join: 24 sc.

Sc in each sc around until Mitt measures 3½" (9 cm) from bottom edge, ending at sc to line up with Ribbing seam.

SHAPING

Markers are used to help distinguish the beginning of each round being worked. Place a 2" (5 cm) scrap piece of yarn before the first stitch of each round, moving the marker after each round is complete.

Rnd 1: Sc in next 6 sc, sc2tog, sc in next 8 sc, sc2tog, sc in next 6 sc; place marker: 22 sc.

Rnd 2: Sc in next 5 sc, sc2tog, sc in next 8 sc, sc2tog, sc in next 5 sc: 20 sc.

Rnd 3: Sc in next 4 sc, sc2tog, sc in next 8 sc, sc2tog, sc in next 4 sc: 18 sc.

Rnd 4: Sc in next 3 sc, sc2tog, sc in next 8 sc, sc2tog, sc in next 3 sc; slip st in next sc, finish off leaving a long end for sewing: 16 sc.

Turn Mitt inside out. Thread yarn needle with long end. Flatten the top of the Mitt with the Ribbing seam at the center of the top edge. Whipstitch top seam *(Fig. G, page 25)*.

Turn Mitt right side out. With **right** side of Ribbing facing, join Black with slip st at seam; ch 1, sc evenly around Ribbing; join with slip st to first sc, finish off.

Weave in yarn ends.

Repeat for second Mitt.

Puffs Blanket

Waves of puff stitches give this lightweight blanket texture and shape. Monochromatic yarn allows the pattern stitch to take center stage.

INTERMEDIATE

Finished Size: 27" x 35" (68.5 cm x 89 cm)

SHOPPING LIST

Yarn (Light Weight) [LIGHT 3]

[2.4 ounces, 282 yards (70 grams, 258 meters) per skein]:

- ☐ 4 skeins

Crochet Hook

- ☐ Size I (5.5 mm) **or** size needed for gauge

Additional Supplies

- ☐ Yarn needle

GAUGE INFORMATION

In pattern,

one repeat (17 sc) and 12 rows = 4½" (11.5 cm)

Gauge Swatch: 9" wide x 2¼" high (22.75 cm x 5.75 cm)

Ch 36.

Work same as blanket Rows 1-6, page 30: 34 sc.

Finish off.

STITCH GUIDE

For a refresher on the beginning stitches, see pages 2 and 3.

DOUBLE CROCHET ***(abbreviated dc)***

YO, insert hook in st indicated, YO and pull up a loop (3 loops on hook), (YO and draw through 2 loops on hook) twice *(Figs. 11a & b, page 6)*.

DOUBLE CROCHET 2 TOGETHER ***(abbreviated dc2tog)*** (uses 2 sts)

★ YO, insert hook in **next** st, YO and pull up a loop, YO and draw through 2 loops on hook; repeat from ★ once **more**, YO and draw through all 3 loops on hook *(Figs. D & E, page 16)* **(counts as one decrease)**.

PUFF STITCH ***(abbreviated Puff St)*** (uses one st)

★ YO, insert hook in st indicated, YO and pull up a loop even with loop on hook; repeat from ★ 3 times **more**, YO and draw through all 9 loops on hook *(Fig. N)*.

Fig. N

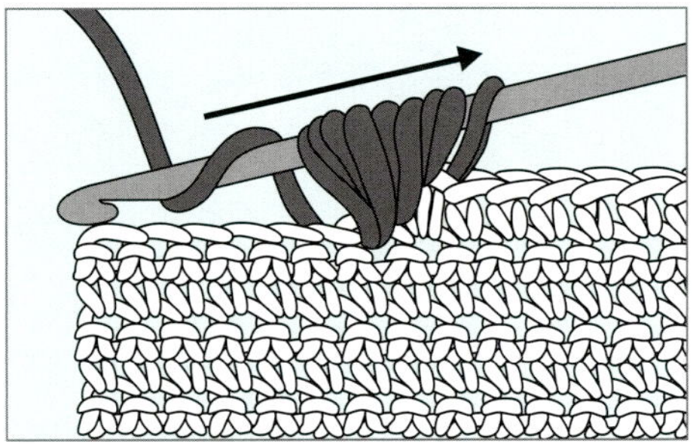

INSTRUCTIONS

Ch 104.

Row 1: Dc in fourth ch from hook **(counts as first decrease)**, dc2tog twice, ch 1, (work Puff St in next ch, ch 2) 5 times, ★ dc2tog 6 times, ch 1, (work Puff St in next ch, ch 2) 5 times; repeat from ★ across to last 6 chs, dc2tog 3 times: 30 Puff Sts, 36 decreases, and 36 sps.

Row 2: Ch 1, turn; sc in each st and in each sp across: 102 sc.

Row 3: Ch 3, turn; skip first sc, dc in next sc **(counts as first decrease)**, dc2tog twice, ch 1, (work Puff St in next sc, ch 2) 5 times, ★ dc2tog 6 times, ch 1, (work Puff St in next sc, ch 2) 5 times; repeat from ★ across to last 6 sc, dc2tog 3 times: 30 Puff Sts, 36 decreases, and 36 sps.

Repeat Rows 2 and 3 for pattern until piece measures approximately 35" (89 cm) from lowest point on beginning ch, ending by working Row 2.

Finish off.

Weave in yarn ends. Block blanket if desired *(see Blocking, page 31)*.

General Instructions

ABBREVIATIONS

ch(s)	chain(s)
cm	centimeters
dc	double crochet(s)
dc2tog	double crochet 2 together
FPdc	front post double crochet(s)
hdc	half double crochet(s)
mm	millimeters
Rnd(s)	Round(s)
sc	single crochet(s)
sc2tog	single crochet 2 together
sp(s)	space(s)
st(s)	stitch(es)
tr	treble crochet(s)
YO	yarn over

SYMBOLS & TERMS

★ — work instructions following ★ as many **more** times as indicated in addition to the first time.

† to † — work all instructions from first † to second † **as many** times as specified.

( ) or **[ ]** — work enclosed instructions **as many** times as specified by the number immediately following **or** work all enclosed instructions in the stitch or space indicated **or** contains explanatory remarks.

colon (:) — the number(s) given after a colon at the end of a row or round denote(s) the number of stitches or spaces you should have on that row or round.

GAUGE

Exact gauge is **essential** for proper size. Before beginning your project, make the sample swatch given in the individual instructions in the yarn and hook specified. After completing the swatch, measure it, counting your stitches and rows/rounds carefully. If your swatch is larger or smaller than specified, **make another, changing hook size to get the correct gauge**. Keep trying until you find the size hook that will give you the specified gauge.

BLOCKING

Synthetics and blends: Submerge project in cool water. Roll piece in a clean terry towel and gently press out the excess moisture. Lay project flat and allow to dry completely, away from heat and sunlight.

Wool: Steam project, supporting weight of iron at all times. Allow to dry flat, away from heat or sunlight.

CROCHET TERMINOLOGY		
UNITED STATES		INTERNATIONAL
slip stitch (slip st)	=	single crochet (sc)
single crochet (sc)	=	double crochet (dc)
half double crochet (hdc)	=	half treble crochet (htr)
double crochet (dc)	=	treble crochet (tr)
treble crochet (tr)	=	double treble crochet (dtr)
double treble crochet (dtr)	=	triple treble crochet (ttr)
triple treble crochet (tr tr)	=	quadruple treble crochet (qtr)
skip	=	miss

Yarn Weight Symbol & Names	LACE 0	SUPER FINE 1	FINE 2	LIGHT 3	MEDIUM 4	BULKY 5	SUPER BULKY 6
Type of Yarns in Category	Fingering, 10-count crochet thread	Sock, Fingering Baby	Sport, Baby	DK, Light Worsted	Worsted, Afghan, Aran	Chunky, Craft, Rug	Bulky, Roving
Crochet Gauge* Ranges in Single Crochet to 4" (10 cm)	32-42 double crochets**	21-32 sts	16-20 sts	12-17 sts	11-14 sts	8-11 sts	5-9 sts
Advised Hook Size Range	Steel*** 6,7,8 Regular hook B-1	B-1 to E-4	E-4 to 7	7 to I-9	I-9 to K-10½	K-10½ to M/N-13	M/N-13 and larger

*GUIDELINES ONLY: The chart above reflects the most commonly used gauges and hook sizes for specific yarn categories.

** Lace weight yarns are usually crocheted on larger-size hooks to create lacy openwork patterns. Accordingly, a gauge range is difficult to determine. Always follow the gauge stated in your pattern.

*** Steel crochet hooks are sized differently from regular hooks–the higher the number the smaller the hook, which is the reverse of regular hook sizing.

CROCHET HOOKS																	
U.S.	B-1	C-2	D-3	E-4	F-5	G-6	7	H-8	I-9	J-10	K-10½	L-11	M/N-13	N/P-15	P/Q	Q	S
Metric - mm	2.25	2.75	3.25	3.5	3.75	4	4.5	5	5.5	6	6.5	8	9	10	15	16	19

BEGINNER	Projects for first-time crocheters using basic stitches. Minimal shaping.
EASY	Projects using yarn with basic stitches, repetitive stitch patterns, simple color changes, and simple shaping and finishing.
INTERMEDIATE	Projects using a variety of techniques, such as basic lace patterns or color patterns, mid-level shaping and finishing.
EXPERIENCED	Projects with intricate stitch patterns, techniques and dimension, such as non-repeating patterns, multi-color techniques, fine threads, small hooks, detailed shaping and refined finishing.

Yarn Information

The items in this book were made using Light Weight and Medium Weight yarns. Any brand of the specified weight of yarn may be used. It is best to refer to the yardage/meters when determining how many skeins or balls to purchase. Remember, to arrive at the finished size, it is the GAUGE/TENSION that is important, not the brand of yarn.

For your convenience, listed below are the yarns used to create our photography models. Because yarn manufacturers make frequent changes in their product lines, you may sometimes find it necessary to use a substitute yarn or to search for the discontinued product at alternate suppliers (locally or online).

WASHCLOTH

Lily® Sugar 'n Cream®

Purple - #01317 Hot Purple

Ombre - #02027 Spring Swirl Ombre

PLAID BLANKET

Lion Brand® Vanna's Choice®

Tan - #123 Beige

Black - #153 Black

White - #100 White

Red - #113 Scarlet

STACKED BLOCKS BLANKET

Red Heart® Soft Baby Steps®

#9600 White

CIRCLE OF LOVE BLANKET

Bernat® Dippity Dots™

#66228 Green

WAVES BLANKET

Caron® Simply Soft®

White - #9701 White

Turquoise - #9608 Blue Mint

FLOWERS & STARS BLANKET

Red Heart® Soft Baby Steps®

White - #9600 White

Red Heart® Gumdrop®

Blue Ombre- #0530 Blueberry

Pink Ombre - #0620 Cherry

Green Ombre - #0625 Apple

BABY HAT

Caron® Simply Soft®

Cream - #9702 Off White

Black - #9727 Black

BABY MITTS

Caron® Simply Soft®

Cream - #9702 Off White

Black - #9727 Black

PUFFS BLANKET

Bernat® Vickie Howell Cotton-ish™

#85315 Cotton Gin

Meet the Designer: Sharon H. Silverman

After many years as a freelance writer specializing in travel books and articles, Sharon Hernes Silverman rediscovered her childhood passion for crocheting and began designing, teaching, and writing. Her fresh designs and crystal-clear instructions have made her patterns favorites among crocheters. Silverman is based in West Chester, Pennsylvania. She blogs at www.SharonSilverman.com and maintains an active presence on Facebook, Ravelry, and Pinterest. She is a professional member of the Crochet Guild of America (CGOA) and a design member of the National NeedleArts Association (TNNA). Silverman and her husband are the parents of two grown sons.

We have made every effort to ensure that these instructions are accurate and complete. We cannot, however, be responsible for human error, typographical mistakes, or variations in individual work.

Production Team: Instructional Writer/Editor - Cathy Hardy; Editorial Writer - Susan Frantz Wiles; Senior Graphic Artist - Lora Puls; Photo Stylist - Sondra Daniel; and Photographer - Ken West.